Toys

Les jouets

leh shoo-*eh*

Illustrated by Clare Beaton

Illustré par Clare Beaton

b small publishing

doll

la poupée

lah poop-*eh*

ball

le ballon

ler bal-*oh*

bricks

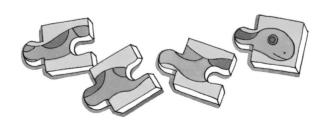

les cubes

leh k'yoob

car

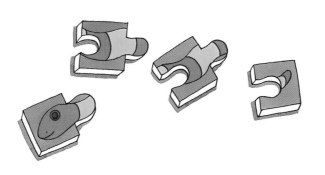

la voiture

lah vwot-*yoor*

fish

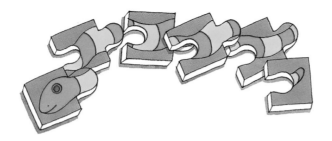

le poisson

ler pwah-*soh*

drum

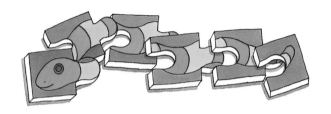

le tambour

ler tom-*boor*

teddy

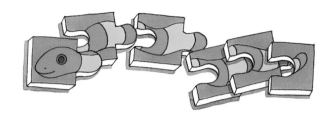

le nounours

ler noor-*noorss*

puzzle

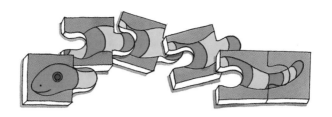

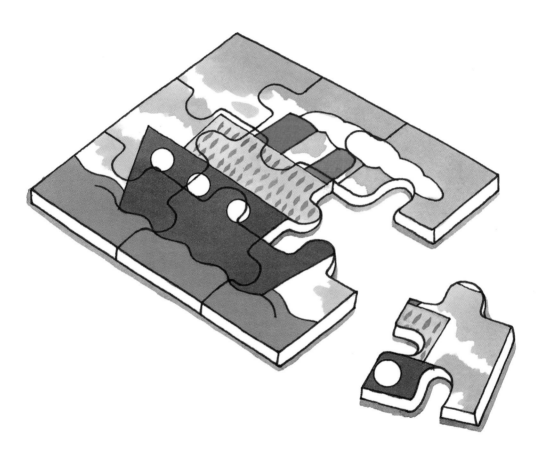

le puzzle

ler perzl'

tricycle

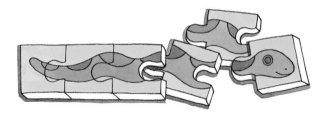

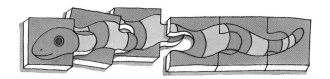

le tricycle

ler tree-*seekl'*

skates

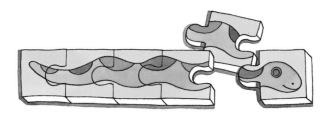

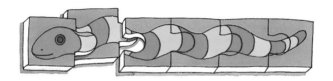

les patins

leh pat-*ah*

crayons

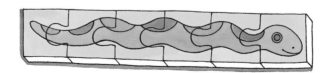

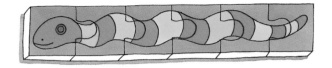

les crayons

leh cray-*oh*

A simple guide to pronouncing the French words

- Read this guide as naturally as possible, as if it were standard British English.
- Put stress on the letters in *italics* e.g. lah vwot-*yoor*
- Don't roll the r at the end of the word, e.g. in the French word le (the): ler.

les jouets	leh shoo-*eh*	**toys**
la poupée	lah poop-*eh*	**doll**
le ballon	ler bal-*oh*	**ball**
les cubes	leh k'yoob	**bricks**
la voiture	lah vwot-*yoor*	**car**
le poisson	ler pwah-*soh*	**fish**
le tambour	ler tom-*boor*	**drum**
le nounours	ler noo-*noorss*	**teddy**
le puzzle	ler perzl'	**puzzle**
le tricycle	ler tree-*seekl'*	**tricycle**
les patins	leh pat-*ah*	**skates**
les crayons	leh cray-*oh*	**crayons**

Published by b small publishing
The Book Shed, 36 Leyborne Park, Kew, Richmond, Surrey, TW9 3HA, UK
www.bsmall.co.uk
© b small publishing, 2003 and 2008 (new cover)
4 5 6
All rights reserved.
Printed in China by WKT Company Ltd.
ISBN-13: 978-1-902915-93-7 (UK paperback)
Cataloguing-in-Publication Data:
A catalogue record for this book is available from the British Library